Notes of a Retired Wedding Videographer

From proposal to reception;
lessons learned from
Brides and Grooms

WRITTEN BY:
C. F. A. Weiss
2006

Bloomington, IN Milton Keynes, UK

authorHOUSE

AuthorHouse™
1663 Liberty Drive, Suite 200
Bloomington, IN 47403
www.authorhouse.com
Phone: 1-800-839-8640

AuthorHouse™ UK Ltd.
500 Avebury Boulevard
Central Milton Keynes, MK9 2BE
www.authorhouse.co.uk
Phone: 08001974150

First published by AuthorHouse 10/5/2006

ISBN: 1-4259-1134-X (sc)

Printed in the United States of America
Bloomington, Indiana

This book is printed on acid-free paper.

Dedicated to all the WannaBe's and Know-it-All's out there who inspired me to set the record straight, and take some form of action against your ignoble and misguided opinions regarding professional videography, the production-quality equipment we utilize, and the level of individual skill it takes to properly pull a wedding video together. Without your lack of research and bad judgment, this book may have never been printed. To you wedding mis-informants I gracefully extend to you a lewd gesture, and thank you for inciting this publication.

To all the already frazzled soon-to-be-married couples: I warmly invite you to read on- so that perhaps you may gain a better idea of what you're in for, where & why things can go awry, and how to avoid having your special day become another nightmarish disaster forever memorialized on video. As a former professional wedding videographer myself, I share with you my insights from so many wedding assignments to contribute to the comfort and success of your wedding day, and to help set the record straight regarding the significance of professional wedding videographers everywhere.

C.F.A. Weiss
2005

TABLE OF CONTENTS

ORIGINS

People have been getting married since society first embraced the institution. Early on, they only had their memories, letters, and verbal accounts through which these memorable events were maintained over time. Soon came portraiture, which only captured a single pose of the newlyweds, and which was sometimes not completed till after their first child and usually at great expense. In the early 19th century photography was invented. Early photography, like portraiture, was merely a single standard pose taken the day of the event, which was then framed and placed above the mantelpiece. As technology advanced and allowed for greater artistic expression via the still image, photographers were able to capture more candid and unstructured scenes. Eventually moving pictures developed and soon thereafter the professional cinematographer. Some of these early cinematographers preferred filming real life events as opposed to the scripted fantasy offered by the movie studios, and thereby provided the basis for the modern documentary filmmaker, and in our case- the Wedding Videographer. The ability to capture the memorable events of a whole day as it happened, and then compile it into to a story-like video documentary for friends, family, and loved ones to view and review again and again- so that the account of that significant event might live on. A hybrid of half historical documentary & half Hollywood filmmaker, the professional Wedding Videographer came into being.

Videography is a component of wedding planning that is often overlooked by most plans. Couples seem to always remember that they want photos of the day, but never remember that nowadays video plays just as great a part- if not greater- in providing a record of the special occasion. It seems like just before the big day arrives, a light bulb blinks on in their brain reminding them to capture the day as it happens with video. Now, they could always ask Uncle John or Aunt Sarah to do it, and hope it turns out mildly viewable at best. Or they could contract a video professional, with professional background training and professional equipment that has the talent & experience required to yield a broadcast-quality video camera. A professional also knows how to hold, run, and shoot for an editor. There is a terrible misconception that many wedding advisors tell would-be couples is that the video technology involved with these services are relatively inexpensive, easy to handle, & self-correcting; and thereby suggest the expense of professional videographer services should be estimated at under a $1000. They couldn't be more wrong; remember- you get what you pay for.

THE 411:

Technology and artistic talent have merged over the past 15 years to create wedding videos that are actually worth watching over and over again. Due to the competition among videographers, various organizations have been formed to allow videographers to share their common experiences & knowledge of the profession in an effort to ultimately become better at what they do. The old days of analog VHS videos with Porky Pig endings, and those corny outdated video effects (including the sound effects!) have thankfully ended at long last. Modern professional videographers strive for a more timeless & classic wedding video. After all, their name is on it. All actual "artists" want to leave behind is great work, representative of their own dedication to quality, accuracy, and artistic production. Stay away from those videographers who are not "artists", those without the passion & 'eye' for creation, as their final work is often lame & impotent- thereby more so providing a video record of their own professional inadequacies or mistaken choice of spend-thrift wedding planners than a media-worthy video record of a special event. Amateur videographers all have the same signature: that is, they will keep the camera on their shoulder the whole day, capture a bunch of wide angle shots, and throw in the occasional unsteady close up. They will claim it is a documentary style but it is more 'paparazzi' quality- i.e. 'just get the shot' style. Such a sacrifice of quality in the video record is really not worthy of being part of such a special day. The actual professional documentary style moves in sync with the happy couple throughout their day, capturing the little details as well as the big picture, and is unafraid of using a little artistic motion (not all shoulder shots)- for in the end, that's is what life is all about: motion.

When I first started to shoot weddings the only cameras that could record the best image quality weighed around 50 pounds- at least for me it felt that way. By the end of the night during my first few wedding assignments, I lost the use of my right arm from the sheer weight of the cameras-making the drive home afterwards rather humorous. Still, I kept shooting them while studying film and video in a New York City College. After graduation, I took a few years off from weddings and studied post-production at some of the top companies in NYC. Eventually I moved out of NYC to New Jersey and found employment with a wedding video company. Only this time I not only shot the weddings - I also edited them. The company I worked for was an outstanding member of WEVA (Wedding and Event Videography Association, International) and highly sought after for their unique, classic and timeless style. It was during my time there that I really gained the exposure to the brides, grooms, and all the wild unwritten happenings that surround a wedding day. I also slowly developed disdain for encountering the same mundane and repetitive music selections played wedding after wedding after wedding, and the cookie-cutter sense of fashion that every couple selects- yet believe they are so very different from every other wedding in selection of its attire. I have found only 2 color schemes popular today: *Grave-yard Formal Black*, and *Puke-Pastel Tropical Powder.* In such situations all I can do is look at them, and say "Sure, your wedding is different- As special & unique as you both are " in a very dry fashion when asked. It is a half-truth. The people of the day are all different to some degree. But after years of shooting and editing these homogenized weddings I have finally had enough. Too many couples trying to nickel & dime me because of some misguided and speculative article on how inexpensive a video should be, usually written by some divorced or un-marriable desk jockey with a degree in complaining for some yenta-magazine.

In the fall of 2004 I read a very disconcerting article on wedding videography that prompted me to telephone the publisher of the bridal magazine directly. While on the phone, I went through the article sentence by sentence correcting it. He was so impressed with the contributions that he invited me to write something up myself to submit. After it was written, it had to be cropped down a bit in order to fit the allocated space- and since I wasn't receiving any pay for the article, I decided to add to the original work.

Hence the creation of this little book- in a big part due to all the badly researched articles, poorly written wedding book advice; and having become bored-stupid with the monotone white, funeral black, sea foam, soft pink, pastel or sickly poo-brown wedding color schemes, each with the same old brow-beaten collection of love songs- including those by Barry White. It's a shame too, because Barry has an excellent voice, and there was a time when I really enjoyed his songs prior to hearing them every assignment. So in order to regain that joy, I had to call it quits to wedding assignments- for myself, and for Barry.

I wish to share with you some of my own thoughts regarding wedding videography, based on my first-hand personal experiences and observations made during my time as a professional wedding videographer. The funny thing is, no one seems to ever think of the videographer as a planning priority. In fact we are usually considered almost as an afterthought, and assumed to fit easily in any budget. The reality is, we should be booked long before your photographer, and in many cases (a.k.a. small budget) you may not even need to hire a photographer due to the fact that "high-res DV cameras" have become so advanced that photograph-quality still images can be taken from the digital video and printed to any-size photographic paper at higher resolutions than traditional video. If you are interested in this cost-conscious capability, I would ask the video company you are considering to hire if they have the necessary equipment, talent, and experience on-hand to support this feature; and if possible, ask to see examples of their previous still-image assignments. Also, the equipment utilized by professional videographers/ editors to record your wedding day are professional grade & rather expensive - and for most videographers, weddings are their primary source of income. So be prepared to allocate a little over $1,000 or more (intensive video packages will coast over $2,000 and sometimes $4,000) for a real professional, and remember- trying to nickel and dime any professional artisan makes you look cheap. When hiring contract professional talent you get what you pay for, and it is highly insulting to low-ball the more reputable creative-design wedding companies. Guard yourself against being sold on names that say they are "Pro's." By definition- regardless if the talent, experience, & creativity is there- all one needs to be a 'pro' is to be paid for something that the hired person does, themselves. I have come across such companies, only to find they still shoot with outdated home-video quality VHS recorders, are limited to in-camera editing, and never include or incorporate anything outside their given assignment in the finished product. They will only shoot the same-old same-old footage, with limited extra/additional/transitional footage regardless of how significant. The great thing about a real *professional* videographer is that they are literally watching you and all the people you invited for that day- they have the professional talent & experience required to more accurately capture and present the video representation of the entire event, including all involved. In time, videographers experience so many different ways to plan & execute a wedding that they themselves become well versed in *how to* and *how not to* plan & execute a wedding. So here are some insights and information I have gained over the years- presented in no particular order- for all the future wedding planners, brides, and grooms to take into consideration. I have seen far too many weddings become train-wrecks, and I hope to help you avoid all the little things which can contribute to these disasters if possible. "Happily ever after" begins long before the day of the actual wedding; rather, it begins in the orchestration of the wedding planning itself…

WISDOM

Preparing for the Big Day

So by this time, you have either made or received a proposal for marriage that yielded positive results. What a wonderful thing it truly is- that is, of course, until you start sharing the news with family and friends. It is inevitable that there will always be at least one person who will be giving you a hard time throughout the entire planning process. It could be the mother of the bride or groom, or the fathers, or (gods forbid) both. After all, they've already survived their own wedding planning & ceremonies years ago, and will likely inject themselves as the on-site experts wherever they can. Even though the to-be couple may have been dating or engaged for quite some time, it could very well be that in the midst of the loosening effect of alcohol, one parent or another (usually the fathers) may make inappropriate comments about the groom's physical desire for his new wife on their wedding night. This mentality comes out at some point in most weddings, and the father of the bride could become quite pissed-off at the father of the groom; and as the whole thing comes to light at the reception, the burden of offense has resulted in more than one wedding brawl that ultimately ends up with the participants head-long in the very well decorated and expensive wedding cake. It makes for a wonderfully impressive demonstration of the many 'tales of stupidity' that videographers, photographers, bands, DJ's and the wait staff themselves enjoy to share with each other over the course of the next few dull, humdrum, wedding assignments. Yes, the people who have worked many weddings eventually become quite sharp-witted and even calloused over it all. A rhythm forms, and each wedding follows suit. This helps everyone you hired for the day know how much longer they have till they can go home. Which, other than being paid for their time, is the only other upshot to the predictable monotony of most wedding assignments.

On the other hand, there are those weddings when everyone gets along, except for the siblings; or any combination of cousins, aunts, uncles, best friends, etc. No matter who it is, just recognize them for the part they are choosing to play in the event, and plan around avoiding that troublesome few. Don't feed into them, as it really only makes them worse- especially if you call them on it. One bride I worked with did confront her best friend on her disruptive behavior. Unfortunately, she was also the maid of honor- that is, up until a few days before the wedding. The story as I was remember went something like this:

The Bride-to-be and the maid-of-honor had been friends for years and of course supported each other though many rotten dates, broken hearts, etc. One night the two went out and the maid spotted the future groom first and made her play. In fact- many plays during many occasions. However, the groom only had eyes for the future Bride. He had mentioned this to the maid several times until she finally seemed to understand and back down. Things seemed to be going great with the happy couple until they announced they were to be married. Throughout the entire planning process, the maid had a passive aggressive and negative undertone throughout her execution of duties. The closer the day came, the worse she became in kind; until the bride finely turned to the friend and went off. She let loose all of her observations and anger toward her dearest friend who had been behaving like a two year old who wants to have it all her way. This display occurred at the seamstress's office with all of the other bridesmaids as well as the mother of the bride present. Good thing too, for there was a bit of a slapping match which had to be stopped quickly before it devolved any further. A few days later on the wedding day, a different friend was the maid of honor. Although the bride was a bit saddened about the behavior of her former friend and how she handled it, the bride had a great day. In her own words she stated, "I feel as if a weight or dark cloud has left me."

If you find you have a substantial resistance working against your marriage intentions, perhaps you should sit down and truly listen to what they have to say; then analyze it, and seriously consider their points of view. There are many sides to a truth. Perhaps your loved ones witnessed something that you should know prior to walking down the aisle. An appropriate wedding toast I have long remembered applies here: *"Marriage is like war: easy to get into, very costly to get out of."* So be sure you both are doing it for the right reasons, and follow your heart- just remember that you don't have to leave your brain behind.

After announcing your intent to march down the aisle, you face the next challenge: *the planning process.* Who to call first? What can we afford? and What is the best price? It is best to settle the location of the ceremony and reception first. This way you have a definite date and location to relay to the other companies you will be hiring. Once you have the date and location selected, then the rest of your decision list can begin. You'll want flowers, cake, food, band for the ceremony and a band or DJ for the reception (and yes, of course a worthy videographer). Due to the busy schedules of photographers and videographers (especially the better performing ones), it is best to book them early on. If you wait until 3 months before the wedding, you will likely have a hard time reserving a videographer of production quality.

CHOOSING YOUR WEAPON (AKA SELECTING YOUR VIDEOGRAPHER)

When seeking a videographer or photographer, contact as many as you can. Ask friends and family, look in the phone book, wedding magazines, ask wedding planners, etc. During their interviews, ask to see examples of their previous assignments and clips from the final videos. Ask photographers which videographers they like to work with and why- for these first-hand referrals help both professional services to produce even better work. Photography and Videography are two different disciplines, each with it's own technology, even though they both share a common, often the same, history.

Most importantly, be leery of video chop-shops that offer to shoot your wedding for ridiculously lower prices than other companies. Nobody ever wants to rewatch videos squeezed-out by these kinds of outfits. You may also lose a few friends if you force them to watch it again, after having survived it the first time. Chop-shops have ruined a number of wedding day memories due to lack or shortage of footage, bad lighting & camera setup, and sometimes even showing impatience with the bridal party and guests. A true professional of wedding videos is not only equipped with cameras that can handle low light, but also knows how to work with the available light; and if necessary then uses a camera-mounted light at low levels so as not to blind or annoy you or your guests.

Here are 5 points of interest you should be aware of when looking at videographic services to hire:

- ∞ Videographers are more likely to offer you a DVD than a VHS copy of your edited final video. It has a longer shelf life and for most, are easier to make. VHS tapes have a shelf life of 10 to 15 years and ultimately fail due to the breakdown of the magnetic coating on the tape itself- even when stored in protected environments.

- ∞ Make a point to find out the caliber and variety of equipment the videographer has invested in. All professional videographers use multiple digital cameras of different sizes and capabilities for various shots. They should all have one thing in common though: "Broadcast quality video" a.k.a. 3CCD. And remember- size does not matter when it comes to camera quality. If you find a videographer that is dead set on 'bigger the equipment, the better', it is a safe bet they will be toting around a bunch of unnecessary & outdated equipment to/from/around your wedding for public display, thereby wasting more time not recording rather than effectively using it, as well as redirecting attention more towards themselves and the camera bulk than what the person has been hired to video.

∞ Find out how many weddings they do a year. If they do over 20, ask if they use subcontractors to cover the jobs they cannot handle themselves. If they do, ask to see their work as well, and definitely meet them in person before the big day.

∞ Ensure the videographer has a wireless microphone system. Most brides and grooms tend to speak their vows very softly. Use of a microphone helps the ceremony sound better on video, and allows you to relive your vows with great clarity. Most videographers will also place a microphone atop the reader's podium. Only there are times, usually during outdoor weddings, when the readers just stand where they are seated, and are never microphoned because neither the bride nor groom informed the videographer of their intended setup beforehand.

∞ Remember to find out if the videographer has only a predetermined amount of recordable media they use for each wedding, or if they have surplus media readily available. The standard recording packages usually offer 8 hours of shooting time, which only includes between 3 to 4 hours of video footage. Any additional footage beyond this will likely occur at additional & unexpected expense. If you are planning on a budget, it is best to pay special attention to the fine-print of the contract package & service details beforehand.

Once you officially contract a videographer, be sure to go over the day's event schedule with them, as well as identify any additional special people that you want to ensure are included in the video. For instance: special vows, your sibling the soldier, someone with a birthday the same day of the marriage, etc. These are events both you and a professional videographer will want to capture. After all, it is only happening on that day, at that time & place, and a number of attendees will likely wish to see it again on video. The video footage provides an excellent way to remember that day and everyone involved. Another detail to address with the videographer is whether they include table shots in their footage or not. Keep in mind, not everyone will be out on the dance floor, and great Uncle Sid may be off in a quite corner of the room sharing stories of the family with others. And it wouldn't be a party without great Uncle Sid, would it? These unplanned gatherings always provide very interesting and enjoyable memories from a different perspective that the special couple would have otherwise missed completely.

When it comes to fees & payment; many videographers will not begin to record until they have received at least 70% to 90 % of the total quoted price of the assignment. The final payment should not be made until after you have the final product, preferably on DVD format.

Try not to overlook the obvious, often assumed, costs which can occur when contracting videographers, photographers, or bands/DJ's, including: meals for the contracted help and crew, travel fees related to non-local or city locations, payment processing fees, final project expectations / amendments / addendums / cancellation fees. Yes, every now and then a wedding is canceled. During a busy season, your wedding date is worth quite a bit of money to your contractors, especially if they have had to turn down other assignments to ensure their availability for yours. It is a good idea to cover the unpleasant subject before you sign the final agreement.

The Big Day

"Where to get married?" This is the biggest and sometimes most difficult decision to make. People of faith tend to want (or have their parents tell them) to have the wedding in a church, synagogue, temple, etc. Wherever it is ultimately held, make sure to find out if the establishment will allow photography and videography to occur during the ceremony. If it is allowed, make sure to clarify the acceptable proximity range to the target for any hired help. Many a Methodist and Jewish establishment will absolutely prohibit such things taking place during the ceremony. Then there are some Episcopalian, Catholic, Baptist, and other Jewish establishments which will allow a videographer to only film from the balcony, while the photographer is allowed to take position in one of the furthest back pews. Most Catholic churches will allow your hired-help to move about during the event, freely and with no restrictions. This is just another detail to clarify before securing the location with any payment or signed contract.

Some couples choose to have both their wedding and the reception in the same location. All wedding contractors and I love such weddings. All too often, somewhere between the Church and reception hall, a videographer or photographer or guest (and once even the newly married couple!) falls prey to Murphy's Law; usually involving accidents, flat tires, traffic jams, lost keys, lost directions, hurricanes, tornadoes, and lions & tigers & bears... Here's a tip: "K.I.S.S". For the all-in-one weddings, I find that the Jewish tradition of a *Chuppah* makes an excellent alter. Now if only some others would catch on. I have seen non-Jewish weddings where the party walks up to a blank space just filled by the justice of the peace and the bridal party. (Boring Sydney! Very Very Boring!) On the other hand, a *chuppah* is a special spot designated for the exchange of vows, and is often visually stimulating and highly ornate, so long as it is dressed well. Few are just a simple arch; many others are a more traditional canopy consisting of four posts with a top draped in wedding cloth and flowers. Although flowers are great at weddings, they are also rather expensive. Alternatively, I have seen lovely lengths of material used as flowing banners- usually white, sometimes red or yellow, depending on the religion and taste of the couple. This adds a romantic sense to the day and the *chupah*; and when mixed with a few strategically placed flowers, really makes the reception area impressively beautiful and cost effective.

Most couples have an easy time identifying the right person to perform the wedding ceremony. They can be from a traditional place of worship as well as found at most wedding reception locations. Many of these reception locations, which also provide the ceremony facilities, maintain a list of Justice of the Peace who are available for that location. It is generally easy to find the right qualified person to conduct ceremonies as long as you maintain affiliation with a mainstream religion; however, if you are a member of a non-institutionalized or otherwise "Pagan" religion, identifying and securing a proper master of ceremonies can be quite a challenge. For instance I know of a couple that had different alternate religions. One was a Viking, and the other a White Witch. It took them over 6 months to find an available Viking priest & corresponding retinue. Unfortunately, even after a calendar year of actively searching, they never were able to find a High Priestess to perform the White Witch wedding ceremony. (Just imagine if all the officers of your religion were shunned, ostracized, hunted down, and even burned at the stake! –because of their beliefs.) In any case, after the proposal and the acceptance, be sure to decide on the religious affiliation (if any) of the ceremony, the ceremony location, and the person to perform the ceremony without delay. After all, for hundreds of years these three components were all that were needed to get married. In my grandparents day they were married at the local church in front of their family and friends, then went home and shared a celebratory meal with a smaller number of people. Eventually post-wedding receptions evolved out of these kinds of simple traditions, and over time evolved into large (often expensive) parties that the happy couple and/or their parents host in celebration.

Selection of the wedding dress, the bridesmaids' dresses, situating the outfits of both soon-to-be Mothers-in-law, dealing with both Fathers' intended outfits; oh yes -and the groom's men's' outfits are often a huge headache that many a bride has suffered through. A few tips to avoid the above include:

- ∞ Always bring a camera while trying on dresses.

- ∞ When trying on prospective wedding dresses, wear simple no-frills underwear and equip boustieres with detachable straps, because some dresses will require too much imagination as to how it will look when you finally do it up right.

- ∞ First time brides tend to pick white for their dresses, that is- unless you are following Middle Eastern traditions (in which case you might likely be swathed in red and gold silks, and have a wedding so beautifully colorful and vibrant that the day really feels electric). The few Middle Eastern weddings that I have been hired to video have all proven themselves to be full-day celebrations of family, love, and happiness with such visual vibrancy and life to capture that to miss even a minute of footage would be a shame. (Without question, they were also some of the most exhausting days of physical labor due to the length and constant motion throughout the event.)

- ∞ One of the most common bridal dresses is the column, or strapless dress. On some brides, it looks great; for most others it looks pretty stupid- especially, if the bride has not practiced how to walk in the long, full-skirted dress before the wedding day. (If they had, they would have realized that the dress constantly feels like it is falling down. Therefore, it needs to be very tight around the waist and taped to the body. By doing this they not only become accustomed to the shallow breathing style, but also tend to less habitually want to pull the dress up repeatedly throughout the entire event. All too often I see brides and maids pulling their dresses up because they feel it slipping down their chest, and fear flashing the room of relatives and friends. Later in the editing process, brides will often ask the editor to cut that repetitive footage out. *Sorry girls- No go.* You should have lacquered it to your body and strutted around your best-friend's house a few times before game day. If you don't, you are sure to see yourself constantly pulling your dress up throughout the entire video.

A note on practicing how to move in your wedding dress: Some brides chose the 'Moulin Rouge' boustiere style which requires you to slowly let it adjust to your individual shape before synching it up really tight. Others chose the 'Queen Elizabeth II - the early years' style, which just requires more tape, glue, and staples if you're up to it. Whatever you do while sizing or styling, be sure to wear light protective clothing between you and the dress, and throw some sheets on the floor so there is no chance of dirt marking up your dress as it drags around behind you. Also, be sure the dogs and cats are not within petting distance of you and your dress- especially if they unconsciously tend to drool, slobber, urinate, or even worse. You want the dress looking crisp and never-before-touched when you walk down the aisle. You can get all the kissy-kissy and make-up marks on it you want afterwards while dancing with the guests, hugging Aunt Rosie, or even setting free little Ernesto (the incontinent ring-bearing Chihuahua) at the reception.

Since I have yet to be a bride myself, I like to ask all of the women who are either in their planning phase or have already walked the aisle, how did they decide on their wedding dress? Too often, I witness a bride wearing the thinnest, spaghetti-strapped or column wedding dress, hardly suitable to wear outside anytime from early November to early April, the coldest part of the year-especially without any kind of pretty bride's coat to keep them warm. Instead they try to "Jedi mind-trick" their own body into thinking they are fine. Meanwhile, the photographer is getting his exterior shots with a bride who is slowly turning blue and beginning to show the telltale signs of hypothermia. Yes, still to this day many brides walk down the aisle knowing that they have "something old, something new, something borrowed, and something blue." (Don't let the 'something blue' end up being your fingers or toes!) Others take tradition further by placing a pence in the bottom of their shoe, or follow other religious and or ethnic traditions. The couples that do thorough research of wedding traditions really impress me; and unsurprisingly tend to have very well thought out and smooth running wedding days. In any case, if you pick a date during a cold month, then stick to that idea and make it work. Christmas-themed weddings are very beautiful, and wonderfully colorful when proper thought is given to it. I have also seen fall weddings done with Squash, both tall and short artistic twigs, rustically done up with the outcome being elegant. Unless you have the thousands of dollars to buy the amount of flowers you would need to make a winter wedding look springy, don't do it. Winter weddings that can only afford the sparse touches of spring flowers tend to look just that way- *sparse* or otherwise *lacking*. Pick a date and match the dress & color scheme that best corresponds to the season. Have fun with the colors of that general time of year. I have seen several beautiful 'snow bunny' brides. While outside they have a layered, luscious, warm look to them. When they are inside, a few layers are taken off, thereby revealing a bride with a working brain. Congratulations, girls- there still may be hope for the rest of us yet...

It is very rare to find a bride who decides on vibrant red for her maids to wear. In fact, now that I think of it, I have only shot three brides who have done so. I'm not going to count the other five because they chose a dark murky red, or merlot- each slight variation of which represent very different meanings. Yes- for people like myself who have worked many weddings, the choice of color of the maids' gowns' reflects the true feeling the bride holds for her betrothed. Check out the movie "The Wedding Planner." Professional wedding planners have a more complete listing of all the colors and their meanings, though they do not regularly advertise this fact. As party planners, they will be running into the bride for many years down the line and often observe how different couples grow together or apart over time. More often than not, the colors included in the wedding give a big hint as to the likely outcome of the couple's relationship down the line. Knowing the chosen colors also helps the planner understand the person's frame of mind. Color is a science that countless amounts of time and money have been dedicated to. It is rare, but every once in a while (and many many wedding assignments later) even a videographer can develop an awareness of these trends. So, as examples of this psychological color wheel in action, here are a few observations I have made during my previous professional experiences. Enjoy.

The Shit-Brown Bride

The first bride that comes to mind is the only bride I have ever seen do this. She had bridesmaids that ranged in size of 2 to 20. The bride picked one style dress for all of them to wear, which of course means the very large girl is *SOL*. However, in this case due to the choice of color involved, they were all out of luck. There is *chocolate* brown, which I do like, and then there is *shit* brown. Chocolate brown is a color of passion, happiness, long devoted life with a good foundation to build on and grow. Shit brown is murky, sickly, with a hint of an odd greenish color and in no way matches rich chocolate brown or even milk chocolate. The maids' dresses' all had this horrible, long-sleeved single piece shit-brown top, made even more offensive & distasteful by being adorned with cheap, gaudy gold trim. The backs of all the dresses were open and deep; a dress design that nearly peeled off the large girl who was forced into it. The skirts of the dresses had horizontal stripes, which would make even *Collista Flockhart* look fat. The color of the horizontal stripes alternated, which can only be described as something like a merry-go-round of shit brown, murky dirty dark purple, and some kind of moldy ill-conceived pink, with each strata separated from above & below by a vein of the same gaudy gold trim which had spread to the long-sleeved top. The bride looked great that day, though the flowers were few, and everyone knew that the bride subscribed to *the very old and antiquated theory that the bride must always be the most attractive female present,* even if this involves an intentional 'dressing down' of the maids. I'm so happy that brides have (for the most part) stopped doing this. The shit-brown bride and her groom were married for a few years and then divorced. A few years later, he met another woman and married again. His second bride had only one maid in a beautiful and lively multi-toned pink plaid dress, which was cut to fit, and looked stunning. They are still happily married and enjoying their first child.

Beware of the Horrors of Sea Foam

Sea foam, although a nice color when getting married by the ocean, is otherwise to be understood as a *kiss of death* color if chosen for a non-seaside ceremony. Any color that reminds one of the colors often associated with gangrene or infection, injuries, murky or swampy, filthy or unhealthy, etc., just screams out that there is something definitely not right with the current picture. Personally, I'm still on the fence with pastels. It could just be a sign of the bride being weak or meek in nature. Not sure why, but Britney Spears' song "Not Yet a Woman" always comes to mind when I see pastels.

The Royal Palette

I have found that the brighter, stronger, clearer royal colors seem to always reflect the strong, clear, long lasting feelings between couples which stand the test of time. Recently a friend of mind was trying to decide what color to pick for her brides maids. She had many people telling her what they think. I merely asked, "What are your favorite colors?" Rich purples, and yellow as it turned out. Her maids will be wearing bright yellow dresses, and be holding a bouquet with purple in it. Easy decision, and the rich, deep, bright yellow dress is a healthy color, and the royal purple with a possible mix of lavender simply luscious. (A note of clarity here, rich royal yellow should not be confused with light sickly pastel or pee yellow. They are two different colors, which leave very different impressions.)

Penguin Weddings

I have also had the misfortune of witnessing black and white weddings. Only one did it reasonably well, with the stronger color being white. Obviously, white represents purity and innocence, and is usually a color of choice for weddings. Black is a color of death, formality, and gravity- and usually found at funerals and other 'weighty' formal events. I must mention that in the Asian cultures the meanings of Black and White switch. Black is pure, and White is sorrow. Then there is the dating mindset of the color Black being mysterious. Only it seems to be over played and drifts into laziness and/or fear of color. Suggestion: check out the many websites about the subject of color and it's meanings as well as the vast amount of books written by accredited people who have made a life study on the subject of color. Since I was born and raised in the Mid Atlantic, I have a real pet peeve about wearing black to weddings. If I am a guest, I choose to wear a color of life and joy. If I am a hired hand, I will wear chocolate brown, gray, or some other neutral color scheme. Some videographers may disagree with this, and feel that, professionally, only black should be worn. This reminds me too much of the *wannabe-Warhol* type of Videographer. Since I don't want to be seen as a black spot on the happy couple's day, I stay away from black. I also tend to wonder about the guest who did wear black to the wedding. Especially, when they add a black hat with a black veil to the whole ensemble. Not to many people notice such things. Sometimes the people who commit these kinds of fashion *faux pas* don't realize the influence they have either. Times like that I have to wonder if it is just a subconscious (or in some cases a conscious) decision to make such a morbid statement simply by their presence and appearance.

Another Penguin wedding I witnessed as a videographer had an almost even mix of black and white. The bride had a white gown with thin lines of black embroidered design on her dress. The maids had black dresses with thin white embroidered design around the top and bottom of there full length dresses. The bride held a bundle of red roses, and the maids held smaller bundles of mixed white flowers. The groom wore a white jacket with black lapels, white tux shirt, black tie and pants. The grooms men wore a black tux with a simple white rose on their left lapel. It was so well balanced that the color scheme reminded me of the Chinese Yin and Yang.

Then there are the antique Penguin weddings were the bride chooses a cream dress. A black and cream wedding has an air of antique love, and longevity. Only what color to chose for the maids dresses? Finding a dress with cream and black design might be a bit hard. The easiest choice is a black gown with the ability to add a long cream sash. Just beware of the flowers you chose. You would not want your bridle party to look like a bruise wearing black and carrying blue or purple flowers. Try reds, creams, whites, pinks, peach or even orange if you are open to a Halloween theme. Penguin wedding themes tend to limit your choices as soon as you decide on it. For those who are not very color oriented it should be a peace of cake. Only the lovers of color will find much stress and aggravation.

When it comes to finding or choosing a color to wrap your flowers or make any kind of bow/knot for any aspect of your wedding, remember this: in many faiths it is believed that to tie a knot is to bind. Should you be a Penguin bride and want to make sure that there is only good chi flowing your way, avoid black ribbon. Even if the ribbon is around the CD of music that you and your groom made as party favors for your guest. Superstitious? Perhaps. Weddings are full of ritual and superstition.

Its the Little Things

Shoes are considered, but never as much as the purse that will be matched to the dress. Shoes are a small element of the day for all members of the bridal party, yet during the day of the wedding; they tend to make the greatest impact, unless you have all the ladies walking down a sandy beach (or in general for whatever reason) completely barefoot. Of course- that would probably be frowned upon if taking place in a church. It is very rare that a maid or even the bride can find a guest who has equipped themselves with suitable shoes to stand in, let alone lend them out to foundering (yet fashion conscious) brides and bridesmaids who have become so hobbled by their tight, pointy, unbroken-in high heels that they barely- and with great pain- made it down the aisle or were able to stand through the brief exchange of vows. I have witnessed some punk rock brides who wear white Doc Martins, or similar boots and non high-heeled shoes down the aisle and throughout the day, without pain or discomfort. It seems that is a great choice. Ladies- remember to pack a pair of comfy run-around shoes so you can better conserve your feet for when you really want to strut your stuff down the aisle. If you are a warm weather bride, strappy sandals seem to be more appropriate. I have seen every heel height from 1" to 8" stilettos worn down the aisle. By the time they make it to the reception, the shoes have either been kicked off or replaced by white, flat, bridle flip-flops. Some brides, or brides' mothers, girlfriends, aunt's etc. get creative and decorate these to match the dresses, or add a bit of special sparkle to them. It may sound corny, but it does make for good video, and usually a little 'macaroni-&-glitter' wind up being very cute, functional, and most of all- comfortable.

<u>The Bonnie Bride</u>

What if you're a couple who wants to incorporate or celebrate your Celtic Heritage during your big day? Well, not only are these types of weddings memorably fun, but also far too uncommon. A tip for anyone who will be renting a kilt: though it pains me to break tradition here, wear something under it. Particularly for the groom's men who are unaccustomed to the intricacies and considerations of wielding a mighty kilt for the first time, does the above apply. Also, keep in mind that rented kilts have been already worn "traditionally Scottish" many times before and by many other renters. (Just something to think about.) Here are a few pointers to be aware of while in a kilt:

- ∞ Know your kilt- especially the weight of the material you select. Heat rises, and kilts are surprisingly warm indoors and out. A medium-weight wool is most suitable for nearly all occasions. Reserve a light-weight wool for summer and a heavy-weight wool for outdoor November/December/January/February winter weddings; otherwise you might find the poor men either sweating or freezing their jewels off.

- ∞ **Be aware of & correct your sitting posture while in a kilt.** Try not to accidentally 'give it all away' without being aware of it- you know what I mean. Avoid sitting with your knees open or with one leg up with ankle on opposing knee. If you see a male guest seated such that the kilt material covering his lap is taught & flat across his legs, and not bowled in between his legs, this could be very embarrassing- especially if seated above the general audience or on stage. Guys- if you might notice someone somewhere smirking or giggling with a slight blush eying your general direction- trust me, they ain't coming on to you...

☞ Vertical lines-of-sight, staircases, and elevated platforms in general are the major contributing factors to kilt-related "clothing malfunctions" and unintended flashings of the naughty bits. Avoid standing on clear or perforated stairs- the people below you who idly look up or between the slats with their meandering gaze might see an unexpected full moon at 10am.

☞ Be aware of vents, outdoor gusts of wind, and large circulating fans; you don't want your guy to pull a 'Marilyn Monroe'- especially on video. (or maybe you do..☺)

☞ Every proper kilt, including the rentals, must be accompanied by an appropriate *sporran* or "ornate little crotch-purse", which often must be rented separately. Never ever ever allow a groom or grooms' man to wear a non-formal sporran to a formal function.

☞ Avoid jumping, stage diving, and twirling while in a kilt. <u>Absolutely, and under no circumstance, is twirling ever to be allowed.</u> Mind the more 'animated' dance styles while on the dance floor, and again- NO TWIRLING.

༉ Be prepared to answer *the question* repeatedly. And be honest, otherwise you might have to back it up. (You know the one- *Wearing anything under your kilt?*)

Of course, the above does not apply to a true Scotsman- as they not only own & wear their kilts in the 'traditional' fashion, they are quite proud of occasionally and 'accidentally' allowing for a peek up the kilt, just for "shits & giggles" at such formal affairs.

Kilt-equipped guests, as well as the groom, must realize that flashing the Videographer or photographer as a personal gift for the new couple for later viewing comes across as always less than striking. Unless you're wearing a hairy thong or smile-face shorts or some other amusing pair of underware beneath, try to refrain from such personal exposures. Don't obsess with being too critical on matching either. It's plaid- a little bit goes along way, and the more 'gravy' you have (a.k.a a fine single-barrel whisky or scotch), the more plaid and tartan you'll want to have. Tartan Kilts are worn best with plain white tuxedo dress shirts, and plain tuxedo black jackets. If you can afford it, make sure you rent a 'Prince Charlie' jacket, complete with formal vest, to really finish out the outfit properly. By the time your heading down the aisle, everyone will have likely had a few drinks, and not really notice any fashion faux pax details. Once the reception comes around, well, just check weapons at the door- including the little knives that formal kilts, contained in the sporran or calf sheath (Sgian Dubhs). Yes, even the Scottish ladies need be checked for sharp objects.(How do think they fend off the men?)

For Celtic weddings the men tend to wear black jackets with white shirts and their family's corresponding tartan. For the Ho-hum wedding it is basically the same only much less stylized with only black pants to match. Some grooms try to wear all white since it is their day to be 'virginal' as well. Not too many can pull that off without looking like an ice-cream man. Take pictures long before hand in many places to see if this choice works on you. And for heaven's sake, enough with the powered blue polyester suit crap. It is your wedding day, not a 1975 high school prom. Have fun without turning it into a joke. Only so much can be done with the groom's attire for the wedding day. The best groom's dress that I have seen was at a renaissance wedding. He was in white with gold trim and looked fantastic. Granted, that does not go with everyone's wedding theme, but it certainly worked for theirs. If you go Hawaiian, be sure to find a silk Hawaiian dress shirt instead of an everyday Hawaiian shirt. There is a difference, and the shops in Hawaii will help you both on-line and in person to properly distinguish. Just to be clear with the jokers, the dressed look includes dress pants and shoes. No flip flops.

Bridal Logistics

Transportation is also a big decision, and scary thing to look for. There are horror stories from both brides and grooms about many limo services. They too are trying to make a living, and to do so they often double book. So if your wedding day is running 30 minutes or more behind, you may find yourself hitching a ride with your guest. Follow your gut feeling when hiring them. The part of the limo service I notice most is always their appearance. I have seen the usual stretch limos in black or white. I have also seen many brides struggle to get out of the low level vehicles. Everyone knows of the classic cars of yesteryear, that when hired will usually throw in a Champaign toast for free. They are generally excellent because they usually put a red carpet down so the bride's dress doesn't soil while traversing the asphalt & sidewalk. Then there are the busses, or extended vans that are adequate to shuttle around your bridal party, yet look cheesy and cheap when one sees a bride exit from one. Granted, the bride may make her exit from the vehicle with little or no struggle, but somehow it just doesn't cut it. In one case, I have also seen a full size touring bus deliver a bride to the church. Still, it may be great for the dress, silly looking, but carries with it a questionable meaning for the marriage. The best solution that I have seen to transport a bride, as well as maintaining her dress, has been a stretch Hummer limo. Rugged and tall which allows the bride an easy exit, and spacious enough to keep her dress from wrinkling, which could also very likely carry the whole wedding party if needed. They too have been known to do a red carpet toast, but as memory serves they charge extra for that.

Awkward Moments

There is always an awkward moment which seems to take place somewhere between the marriage ceremony and the reception at every wedding. For example: If you're coming out of a place of worship, where do you stand to greet your guest? Or should you even stop to greet them at all? And while in transit between sites, how to handle the guest who relentlessly keep blowing bubbles throughout the champaign toast or incessantly throwing almonds at you in accordance with an old Italian wedding tradition? Some facilities have a nice inner foyer leading into the actual religious space. This is the ideal spot to stop and greet guests- this way they can wait outside for your grand exit without contributing to uncomfortable traffic congestion. It also makes for a great wide-angle shot in the video when you exit the ceremonial building with all your guests smiling as they throw rice, almonds, coins, or whatever at you. Again, religious and sometimes ethnic backgrounds can come through very clearly here as well. There are still some couples that follow the old tradition of jumping over a broomstick after being announced as husband and wife. So be sure to make room! This cultural tradition has been in practice long before the Civil War. Regardless of the space you have to work with, it is always best for the bride, groom, and everyone in the wedding party to just keep smiling no matter what- even if stung by a bee. So be sure to break out the ChapStick, moisturizing lip-gloss, or the old Miss America trick of smearing Vaseline over your teeth & lips, as you'll all be marathon smiling all day. Remember, the cameras are always rolling: capturing every emotion, every word of your physical language; and the microphones are recording all the expletives that usually are uttered beneath one's breath. As long as you smile, the photos and the music that are incorporated into the final cut will never show the true "S&%**" that is going on.

The following awkward moment is not so noticeable for a one-location day. The guests are ushered to the cocktail room, and the photographer and videographer pull you outside to take a few special shots- that is, unless you're Jewish. It is tradition for the Jewish bride and groom to meet before the wedding and perform a "Is this the woman you promised to marry?" ceremony. Formally known as a Bedekin. There is an old Jewish story of how a man married a woman thinking it was the one he wanted, only it turned out to be her ugly sister. Since then, it is common for the couple and their closest family to meet, sign an illuminated manuscript equal to a work of art called a Ketuvah, for the modern orthodox lift the vale where the traditional orthodox perform a Bedekin where the vial is placed over the brides face by the groom, sing a ceremonial song, and get on with the day. Between that and the actual wedding, the photo and video are then taken which allows the happy new couple more time with their guests and to enjoy a sit-down meal. Many brides have told me they did not eat a thing for most of the day and wound up finally sitting down to dinner at 24 hour McDonalds, or eating a load of airline peanuts while *en route* to their honeymoon destination. Other brides (aware of this) have made time to sit down to eat, thereby bringing the guests to them. And even others have the wherewithal to have their reception at a five-star hotel, complete with a restaurant for the guests and a honeymoon suite with room service waiting for them.

Some hotels will even include a free bottle of Champaign with the meal. Whatever you do, it 's best to consider this in advance. It may not seem like a big issue beforehand, but when the big day arrives- with lots of drinks being poured down your throat, with little or no food in the belly, and your feet about to give out on you- a little forethought will provide ample comforts.

DJ or Not to DJ

Many couples may have a difficult time deciding on either a DJ or a live band. I have experienced each individually at a wedding, as well as both at one wedding. In my opinion, I would opt for both on a wedding day, if it were in the budget. The reason for this is *continuity of flow*. When the band takes a break, the DJ kicks in, providing for either a continuation or transition of the musical ambiance based on the mood of the crowd or progression of the party. It also allows your guests to identify the original composer/performer of the song, in most cases always sounds distinctly better in its original version than in any remake or cover-band performance. If your budget can't afford both, then go with a DJ who includes a light show. Lots of fun, good dancing, and the colorful light show helps get people to the dance floor. Just remember that any photos or video taken during the light show will very likely be unexpectedly colored in the final print, even when taken on the most expensive professional video or photo equipment. Expect your depth of field to be within 4 feet and mainly consist of a patchwork of close-up baldhead shots, best friends' opened mouths, and boobs nearly popping out of low cut dresses. However, when the floor is full & the mood is high, and the camera has it's own mounted light to counter balance the flashing multi colored show, the final footage taken during the light shows on the dance floor should turn out much more visually appealing.

Wedding Party Announcements

To have the wedding party guests announced or not is a consummate question. On one hand, it is nice to openly recognize those participants who have contributed above-and-beyond expectation to ensure that the wedding is a most memorable occasion. It acts as a kind of "thank you" from the couple to have them announced when they enter the room. After all, they did sponsor the outfits and then chaperone someone they've never met on your behalf. The key thing here is to entrust someone who knows and can accurately pronounce every name in your wedding party with the responsibility. All too often I hear the bridal party speaking among themselves about how their name was butchered by the DJ, Maitre D, Band Leader, etc. It's especially noticeable when a simple name like 'Smith' is pronounced 'Smythe'.

Once you decide if you want a band or DJ it is best to consider the age, and musical taste of your guests. By all means, have a few songs that you and your groom enjoy, only be considerate to the crowd. Whatever you do, please don't choose the usual route of Top 5 80's and 90's hits; everybody plays those songs to death. I had a bride and groom who both loved the oldies- only in order to be different; they played the bottom 100 listing. Even though people were dancing, it eventually made me literally ill. All too frequently I have been present at weddings with little (if any) dancing taking place, even though the music may have been electrifying. The primary reason for this was the age of the majority of guests- older crowds dance less to unfamiliar tunes- and when it comes to post production of the wedding video, this looks utterly pitiful. I find that a nice mix of 1920's Charleston mingled into current music selections popular today helps to get a much wider variety & number of people dancing. Even your youngest guest can't resist the rhythm of a peppy 1920's tune. It also helps your guests to be less inhibited if the bride and groom do a lot of dancing as well. In light of this, I would suggest looking into some formal dance training in preparation. It will help build both your stamina and muscle strength up for your big day. You will also find that seeing yourself on the video dancing with confidence is much more fondly remembered than not.

One would think that from here on in the video is easy. It's not. The photographer and videographer have a few more key things to capture like the dances, speeches, and cake cutting. Usually, they will also try to grab a quick snack during cocktails, since the rations provided for the contractors during these assignments can frequently be described as 'highly unappetizing' at best. By the time all the speeches and dances have been shot, we (the hired help) have usually figured out which of your guests is also a relative pain in the ass, and actively avoid them. These are the guests who either try to jump in a given shot, or flash a light or laser pointer at our lens from across the room. Once the generic dancing starts, these are the guests who also tend to stick their middle finger up at the camera as if they are being original. I never understood these odd-ball relatives & guests; especially because the hired hands are there at the request & expense of the couple. Such vulgar and puerile behavior is often cut from the final video at request of the couple. As a female videographer I have even had such asinine people (usually men) also add to their already impressive array of idiocy by grabbing my breast while I am shooting whatever the bride and groom are doing noteworthy at the time. I have even shot a wedding reception comprised mostly of kung-fu and karate experts; who in their inebriation, proceeded to use my equipment and me as their practice targets. I promptly told the bride that if I get kicked or punched one more time, I quit and they'll be hearing from my lawyers. Keep in mind that photographers, videographer, bands, etc. can bring an unexpected and drastic end to a party should they become negatively involved in the event. No one wants to put up with unruly guests. Some Vendors even put in their contracts that they will leave if repeatedly attacked or harassed by your guests after informing you of the first instance. Others figure it is obvious, which it is- but not always taken care of in time.

At weddings, I tried to blend in as much as possible so as not to annoy the guests or draw too much attention with my camera. This courtesy often resulted in larger portions during cocktails, even at the more upper crust reception halls. Some reception halls have rules against videographers, photographers, DJ's, etc. eating any of the food during cocktail. Depending on the number of security cameras and the need for dietary fiber of the person in charge of the hired staff, they may or may not strictly adhere to this rule. While circulating throughout the evening crowd, frequently I am presented with opportunity when one or more of the guests would like to speak to the camera and say a few words to the happy couple. Some video services promote these impromptu speeches while others don't; and I always just humored them- even if the bride and/or groom actively instruct against such contributions, I still capture it. I remember one wedding in particular, when this unauthorized kind of guest contribution had particular unexpected value. The bride's wild and crazy brother made the contribution. He was in the wedding party, and had to say a few things to his sister and new brother-in-law. A month later he died suddenly in a motorcycle accident. These few seconds of video soon became a very important segment included in their final video. I feel that some couples who are afraid that the Videographer will be chasing guests around like a news reporter intentionally instruct us not to video guests who speak directly into the camera. To avoid this potential loss of valuable contributions, it is always a good thing to discuss with your videographer before hand. If people want to say something, let them. It does not have to be on the final video. You will have the copy of the collective raw footage to replay whenever you want to revisit the unedited day.

Not to darken the mood too much, but we will all eventually keel-over. Some of us are closer to this fateful day than others. Usually as professionals we can figure out who the key people are, yet there are times when you have someone important there at your wedding, only they take no part in the wedding festivities themselves, and maintain a quiet, reserved presence somewhere by the walls and/or safely out of the way. We like to think that each day they will be there for us, yet too often, we find ourselves reminded that life is rarely that predictable or inexhaustible. Make a point to alert the videographer of any additional special guests you would like to have included on the video- because for some, it may be their last evening out; and how thoughtless would it be to have the wedding photos and video overlook them during your special day when it is likely they have been with you throughout your entire life. Respect the elderly, for in many cases they have sacrificed their youth for you…

From Cookie-Puss to Angel food (Its all about the Cake)

The last key element of shooting a wedding is the cake cutting ceremony/event. I have seen many cakes: good cakes, bad cakes, cheap cakes, and even ugly cakes. It doesn't really matter to me (although I did feel for the one bride with the ugly cake. I mean really- how depressing is that- an ugly cake on your wedding day. Even the crowd gave it a second take; you know the look- that look everyone gives to the proud parents of an ugly baby during a stroll through the park.) In any case, either **during cocktails or at the start of dinner is a good time** to catch a few specialty shots of the whole event- in both wide angle and up close in detail. In the final edit with the overall scene put to music, the scene truly comes to life.

I have heard from some wedding planners that the choice of cake also gives a clue into how long a marriage will last. Depending on how 'traditional' the couple's beliefs are, round cake shape represents the infinite; and a square shape has its beginning and ends. It's kind of neat to see a 3-layer square cake done up like a present, wrapped up in that gossamer icing. Before the cake cutting I've made a habit to speak with the person who will be assisting the couple in cutting it. Too often while shooting the cake cutting, the assistant is overly assistant- to the point where in the video it looks more like a cake inspired ménage-a-trois. Both the photographer's assistant and the guests have been seen pulling the cake-cutter-assistor out of the shot. The kicker is that they always end up with such a look of insult. Somebody outta tell them to go and plan their own wedding, and get the hell out of the current wedding's footage.

There is another trend which seems to be a predominantly southern tradition- having a groom's cake. It is very rare to attend a wedding with a groom's cake up north. The times that I have seen it, the groom and his family were southern. The first time I noticed it, was during the wedding of 2 lawyers- both the bride and groom were from the south and both were lawyers in NYC. All in all, it is tradition to have a fancy cake for your cake-cutting ceremony. Long ago it was truly a rare treat to have such elaborate cakes at all, unless you were royalty. Usually fancy cakes or the traditional sweet buns were done for weddings to symbolize the sweetness within the relationship. For those couples that do not enjoy cake, like my cousin and her husband, choose to have the cake anyway, even if only for the symbolic value and fun. My cousin & her beau were initially not going to have a cake at their wedding; that is, until the families of both found out about the decision. It then became a huge issue to both families of how they had to have the cake and perform the cake cutting. Save yourself the unnecessary pains associated with breaking or attempting to break the cake tradition. After all- everybody loves cake. Rather, do what my cousin did: cut your cake on the first landing of a staircase as if it were your stage. After mashing both your faces into it, throw the remainder into the crowd. (just watch out for those friends who can catch such a mess and throw it back at you!) I'm sure the manager of the hall didn't appreciate the extra cleanup, but we all had an excellent time- and that's all that matters on that day. A variety of desserts were then served bufey-style from a designated table in the same room where the cake ceremony had taken place.

Some weddings really go all out when it comes to the desserts. I remember a few wedding assignments in NJ and NY which had even rented antique Venetian desert tables from which the desserts were served. Every inch of the tables were covered in desserts, and there must have been nine tables in all, and every dessert was unique. It was awe-inspiring. This was one wedding where the guests actually ate most of the desserts presented.

At the end of the day's events, photographers will typically pack-up and depart when their hired time expires. Videographers, on the other hand, will be actively seeking the closing shot by which to conclude the video production. Depending on how affectionate and romantic the couple is while being videoed, the videographer may or may not have to prompt the newlyweds to obtain this memorable closing shot. In my mind, the best closing shot is a dipping embrace with a zoom into the kiss. Or if they are (still) on the dance floor having a blast, close-ups of unprovoked twirls or dips accompanied by a kiss also work well. Some guests or hosts like to say something for the closing, or suggest the groom carry the bride through the threshold and off into their married lives. It may sound hokey and old-fashioned, but the visual looks wonderful- and the physical language recorded on video unmistakably communicates such passionate and wonderful things about the new couple to any who would view the video.

Bad Boys & Girls: When Newlyweds Offend

Oddly enough, in my past wedding experiences I have come across grooms who would not kiss the bride, and /or walk the bride (or their mother) to the dance floor. Weddings with grooms like these are utterly doomed. Not to say that the brides are any better- I have also seen brides who refuse to embrace their groom (or openly avoid his embrace), as well as intentionally shy away from their kiss. To the sheltered and bashful newlyweds out there: *You're married now; people have spent a lot of time and money contributing to your special day- Kiss each other already.* If you or your mate *really is* that bashful- then pucker up for the camera now and giggle about it later that evening together. Your wedding day is yours (plural) and yours alone; and not even Papa Bear himself can say otherwise. Still- some newlyweds choose to 'restrain' expressions of their affections for each other, and other newlyweds can't keep their hands off each other. In both cases:

1. This does not present well in the video when the bride and the groom are individually profiled on video without ever being filmed together in the same scene.

2. Even during the last few minutes while the cameras are still rolling, everyone needs to keep in mind that they are still live on camera, and to behave accordingly- no live porno's, Please. Children and ageing people with heart conditions are present.

While on the subject of behavior- during one of my assignments the following actually happened. As I was breaking down the wireless microphone with the camera still connected and recording, it managed to inadvertently pick up what would turn out to be a rather obnoxious & ill-advised conversation involving the newlywed husband. He was quite openly leading a discussion with his groom's men in regards to which bridesmaids he would attempt to have a sexual fling with after the reception. Thankfully, I have only had this happen once in the many years I have been shooting wedding videos, and hope I never have to hear it again. Such inconsiderate and braggart grooms better be damn ready to shell out a few extra bucks to have this video footage "lost", even if spoken in jest or under influence of Cuervo when 'hangin out with the guys' on camera. Some people would immediately inform the Bride- which is neither their place nor their moral right as contracted help; while others might try to leverage the comments/footage for nefarious financial gain. To everyone attending videoed events: Mind your manners, drinking, behavior, and your spoken words at all times. Your on camera, Baby!

Yes Ladies & Gentlemen- I can hear everything you say and do much more clearly than your own ear wax- once you have that wireless microphone on. (You know, the one clipped-on early before the event and have since obviously forgotten about) So please, watch what you say- about others and about myself (the Videographer) in particular. (*To anonymous: I know I have breasts, and have been aware of them for quite some time now- so thank you for complementing their shape, appearance, and fullness during so many lewd discussions with your friends during that wedding assignment. You know whom you are- and I have it on tape. By the way- while you were at it, did you ever explain to your wife why the belt you chose to wear for your wedding had all those little notches? I am certain she would appreciate that.*) Some grooms are very serious about the day, others joke the whole way through. Everyone's weddings are different and unique- save one single universal wedding commonality: regardless of faith, theme, style, or betrothal ceremony involved, everybody breaks for the lavatory immediately preceding (in preparation for?) *the bride's walk down the aisle.* Unfortunately (and to my own horror and to the horror of videographers everywhere), not everyone only *pees.*

Please- for the love of whatever you hold sacred- lay off the beans, oat bran, fast food, *whatever*- to avoid "tooting your own horn" too soon! Gads- What a sound that is in theater-quality Dolby Digital EAX !! Fortunately, these 'extra sounds' can be strategically edited out of the final video and corresponding audio tracks. You and your bride will always have these kinds of treasured memories for years to come, archived on the raw footage to discuss, laugh or fight about.

I should make mention that not all men are necessarily as lewd when enjoying the wedding festivities, and I rather prefer never to give thought to anyone's wedding evenings. I do want to bring to attention the importance of all the wonderful little things the couples share with each other throughout the course of the day's many events, even if in passing or while in the company of only themselves.. and the microphones, of course. Those little whispers of affection like "You look wonderful," or beautiful, fabulous, sexy, etc. is usually mentioned a few times by the groom to the bride. Or how nervous they were until they had survived the ring ceremony; or how they are looking forward to the reception; or how much 'courage juice' they needed before walking down the aisle. Sometimes they will recognize unexpected or particularly special attendees, or what they are wearing or who their date is through sheer body language. Again, the vast majority of this footage is cut out of the final video, yet can still be found in the raw footage. After all, the raw footage is primarily intended for the newlyweds to view- and not for the general audience.

There are good grooms who are deeply in love with their bride, and then there are bad ones who will wander after the first day of being married. The same is true for brides. Only brides are usually the most unruly of the happy couple, especially the day of. Based on my experiences and number of weddings contracted for, it always seemed that the most 'problematic' brides- (i.e. *the whiniest, bitchiest, most ridiculously demanding & caustic poison-filled princesses*) were always the product of an unusually privileged and wealthy background combined with over-loving parents who never taught their monstrous offspring the value of "No", let alone even the basics on how to survive on their own talents. I have even had a few experiences where some princess-brides explode in a spoiled fury of verbal curses and puerile tantrums on on camera at the silliest, most meaningless non-issues! And worse- usually at their own or someone else's mother! Shocking and True! This is again just a generalization, and in my opinion, based on my previous experiences at wedding assignments. For the majority of us working-folk, as long as there is room enough in the budget for a single wedding planner (or even an organizer just for the day), DO IT. The brides with planners I have captured on video tend to have been less stressed and more time to really enjoy their day.

It is important for all brides to remember that many men are not interested in the little details that go into planning a wedding. One groom I know summed it up best with, "I found my Bride, We have the church, priest, transportation, and reception hall that is handling all of the food. Planning done." This didn't surprise me, the Bride was.

Many grooms feel this way and it is not meant to be an attack on the Bride or their relationship. Granted it would be great to find one of the few men out there who do become very involved in the planning process. Guys are good at the big planning and lean on their beloved to handle the little things. After all, most women are good with little details. We have also been planning our wedding day since we were little girls. So enjoy those little details and the full control you hold over them. Just keep in mind his likes and dislikes and you can't lose. Should you find that you need your groom to make a call or pick something up, just ask him in a nice way to do the task and put "it" in a common spot for you to find. Your groom loves you and wants to do everything for you. Just remember that words and the tone that they are spoken in can lift one's soul to heaven or plunge it into hell. There will be stresses in planning such a big event, so try not to take it out on one another.

If the budget is really not there, ask one of your friends to take over the execution of the wedding ceremonies. Just remember to give your kind friend or family relative a complete list of your vendor's names, functions, and contact information. Also include a detailed list of how you want the day to run with start and end times. No detail is too small. The more information they have to see to a smooth execution of the day's events the better. It might also be a good idea to give them your cell phone for the day. That way should the vendors try reaching you due to a traphic hold up, they will reach your first in command for the day. It will also alleviate the stress of the day on you. Remember, a bride who has an overly stressed wedding day will never have the chance to truly enjoy it.

The Wedding Toasts

One of the best wedding toasts I have ever heard was at an Indian wedding. The Uncle addressed the newlyweds with microphone in hand and advised, "Never go to bed angry. Stay up and fight!" He is absolutely right. Communication is the key to any good relationship of any kind. Speak your whole mind, and speak from your heart. If something that someone does hurts or offends, tell them. If you feel your life's path taking you someplace, then say so, and try to include your partner, even if they can't go along for the journey. Real mind-readers are few & far between since dragons died out, so if you choose not to speak up, you have only yourself to blame- not the other person. Smile often, and look for the humor and folly in things- because the negative is all-too-easy to find anymore and can easily poison your new life together.

After the big day (and the big night!), some new wives rush out to have their names changed; others just append their husband's surname to the end of their maiden names, winding up with an oddly disjointed and very long full name through which to identify themselves. Then there are those who don't make any changes at all. Ultimately, it all comes down to personal preference. When looking back in history, especially in the Native American Culture, men took the woman's name because it is easier to know where the children come from. The Jewish traditions have a similar religious tradition to this day: if the mother is Jewish, then the baby is Jewish.

The truth of the matter is- we all choose whom we marry; let us then make wise decisions with whom we choose to share our lives with- from babies to bank accounts, from fart jokes to funerals, and from the birth to the passing-on of all which you together cultivate within your new little world called "Us". Remember the value and strength of body language & physical contact. When the physical intimacy or communications cease- the foundations of the interpersonal relations shift to much less reliable grounds, prompting more and more selfish & egocentric tendencies to cultivate themselves under the guise of ennobling concerns for the relationship. (It's a personal kind of defensive cop-out, to balance out something missing from somewhere else in the relations.)

IN CONCLUSION

Towards the end of the wedding reception, tips are usually distributed to the contractors either by someone designated by the couple or by the couple themselves. Tips generally go to the Videographer, Photographer, Band, and DJ. Although tips for the wait staff does occur on occasion, it is rare. It is not a mandatory custom or expected, yet it is nice for a subcontractor to receive at the end of a long day and night. A few times this added little bonus has helped me fill my gas tank in order to make it home.

After the wedding day you will likely still have two contractors working for you, possibly 3 if you have the money to keep your wedding planner on in order to pick up the photos and final edited video for you.

The photographer will go through the process of organizing your photos, possibly uploading them to the web so you can choose which photos will be included in your final photo album. This also allows for an opportunity for the couple to select which photos they would like to have portraits made out of. One couple I know had a very large poster size photo of them on there wedding day framed in a thick heavy wood frame. The bride's dress was actually cheaper than this framed monstrosity. It is possible to have your portrait photos any size you desire-just make sure you have a fitting place to hang it first!.

The videographer will process the tape footage at the studio, and either edit it themselves or have a trusted editor do it for them. It is great when you have a videographer who has the capability to both shoot and edit your wedding video because they have greater insight as to how the final production will look and feel (i.e.- since they were there with you). Videographers who do not participate in or understand the editing process would probably want to avoid the poor editor tearing their hair out and trying to make something beautiful and coherent out of the footage the basic videographer provided them with. Some video production companies allow the couple to select their own music for the video soundtracks; others only allow the couple to choose 3 to 6 songs of a few genres for the editor to work with. Sometimes couples even find themselves dealing with a company that offers them no choice in what music is applied to the montages, and can only rely on the quality of a prepackaged selection. It is best to check into these little details prior to signing the final service contract. Even during the final editing process <u>you</u> can still determine to cut any rude remarks, falls, overly frisky grooms grabbing their bride's boob, as well as any other "wardrobe malfunctions" or detracting events to be included in the final footage. It makes for some funny outtakes, but to avoid any further embarrassment of the poor individual, it is best to censor or cut out completely the embarrassing or unexpected event. Some studios will allow for last minute changes by the couple before calling it finished. Others do not. No matter who the studio is, the final payment is expected at the time you pick up the finished product (i.e. edited shortened video of the day to share with everyone, and raw footage as a keepsake or torture device). Some places try to make the final product available within 3 to 8 months, and others could take up to a year. It is rare to find a place that can and will turn it around in a week. I would be highly concerned with what the montage video would look like with such a turn around time- and so should you.

Finally, remember to occasionally revisit your wedding video every once in a while throughout your life; as it provides a visual record of the day your newlywed world was created as well as the beginnings of a long, happy history of your love. Based on its initial atmosphere, environment, natural & inherited resources, and the celestial bodies it orbits- your new world will either prosper or wilt based on the decisions you have both made and have yet to make. And remember- *parenthood is the first divinity* recognized by every child; and especially as creators, we must wholly embrace that which we create, for better or worse- that is each of our own responsibilities, alone and together.

Follow your bliss- it rarely leads you wrong.

Cheers,

CFA

ABOUT THE AUTHOR

Christine F. A. Weiss has been considered a 'shutter bug' since early childhood. She is the daughter of a fine-art /graphics artist who nurtured Christine's interest and involvement in the arts by exposing her to many Philadelphia museums during her childhood. In high school, she won several awards and a number of scholarship from the Moore College of Arts high school higher education program for her talents. The culmination of her successes in fine arts was soon realized by achieving several scholarship offers from numerous colleges and universities, but ultimately she decided to attend a renowned visual arts college in New York City. Using this as a vehicle to gain the industry awareness necessary to make an educated decision, Christine decided to specialize in cinematography and lighting design.

While with Broadway Video she studied the post-production aspect of cinematographic production and was offered the opportunity to learn first-hand what real life professional editorial positions entail. Then, in 2001 Christine relocated from NYC to north New Jersey to advance her career while with Bitcon Productions (a prestigious wedding video company) and IVP New Media (a professional legal video services company). During the interim period between these consultant positions, she honed her skills with the video camera via subsisting solely from filming and editing contract wedding videography assignments, thereby working very closely & in-person with numerous newlywed couples.

In 2003 Christine relocated to Delaware to be closer to her aging parents and establish her own videography services company. Initially, her videography services included both wedding and legal video assignments. However, due to a few too many obnoxious wedding guests and the resulting damaged equipment, she decided to refocus her videography services to the much safer and more sane environment of legal videography...

Made in the USA